General Editors

LYNN Z. BLOOM
University of Connecticut

LOUISE Z. SMITH
University of Massachusetts, Boston

THE ST. MARTIN'S CUSTOM READER

Selections Compiled by

MICHAEL DARCHER
ENGLISH
PIERCE COLLEGE
ENGLISH 101-GW: COMPOSITION

Bedford/St. Martin's   Boston ◆ New York

Copyright © 2001 by Bedford/St. Martin's

All rights reserved. No part of this book may be reproduced, stored in a retrieval system, or transmitted in any form or by any means, electronic, mechanical, photocopying, recording, or otherwise, except as may be expressly permitted by the applicable copyright statutes or in writing by the Publisher.

Manufactured in the United States of America.

7 6 5 4 3 2
f e d c b a

For more information, go to the Bedford/St. Martin's Web site: www.bedfordstmartins.com or write: ATTN: Custom Publishing, Bedford/St. Martin's, 33 Irving Place, New York, NY 10003.

CONTENTS

RUSSELL BAKER, *The Plot Against People* 1

JOHN CIARDI, *Is Everybody Happy?* 4

ESTHER DYSON, *Cyberspace for All* 8

BARBARA EHRENREICH, *Oh, Those Family Values* 13

WILLIAM FAULKNER, *Nobel Prize Award Speech* 16

MILTON FRIEDMAN, *Prohibition and Drugs* 18

PETE HAMILL, *Winning Isn't Everything* 21

SUSAN JACOBY, *Notes from a Free-Speech Junkie* 26

THOMAS JEFFERSON, *The Declaration of Independence* 30

MARTIN LUTHER KING JR., *I Have a Dream* 34

WILLIAM KOWINSKI, *Kids in the Mall: Growing Up Controlled* 38

BRENT STAPLES, *Black Men and Public Space* 43

DEBORAH TANNEN, *Sex, Lies, and Conversation* 47

RUSSELL BAKER

The Plot Against People

In his Pulitzer Prize–winning autobiography, *Growing Up* (1982), Russell Baker (born 1925) explains that his widowed mother determined that he would "make something" of himself. Baker's journalistic career began when she obliged the quaking eight-year-old to sell magazines door to door and encouraged him to become a writer. His literary breakthrough came when he entertained his high school class with a comical essay, "The Art of Eating Spaghetti." Baker trained as a navy pilot during World War II, and he began working as a *Baltimore Sun* reporter immediately after graduating from Johns Hopkins in 1947. In 1954 he joined the *New York Times* as a congressional reporter—a career he describes in *The Good Times* (1989), the second volume of his autobiography. After eight years, "exasperated with the pomposities of official D.C.," as a *Times* columnist he wrote "The Observer," a nationally syndicated satiric commentary to which he still contributes occasionally. In 1993 he began hosting PBS's *Masterpiece Theatre*. In "The Plot Against People" (1968), Baker directs his satire against three categories of things: "those that don't work, those that break down, and those that get lost." Employing the satirist's techniques of exaggeration, ridicule, and personification of inanimate objects, Baker gives cars and women's purses lives of their own.

Inanimate objects are classified scientifically into three major categories—those that don't work, those that break down, and those that get lost.

The goal of all inanimate objects is to resist man and ultimately to defeat him, and the three major classifications are based on the method each object uses to achieve its purpose. As a general rule, any object capable of breaking down at the moment when it is most needed will do so. The automobile is typical of the category.

With the cunning typical of its breed, the automobile never breaks down while entering a filling station with a large staff of idle mechanics. It waits until it reaches a downtown intersection in the middle of the

---

Russell Baker, "The Plot Against People" from the *New York Times* June 18, 1968. Copyright © 1968 by The New York Times Co. Reprinted by permission.

rush hour, or until it is fully loaded with family and luggage on the Ohio turnpike.

Thus it creates maximum misery, inconvenience, frustration, and irritability among its human cargo, thereby reducing its owner's life span.

Washing machines, garbage disposals, lawn mowers, light bulbs, automatic laundry dryers, water pipes, furnaces, electrical fuses, television tubes, hose nozzles, tape recorders, slide projectors—all are in league with the automobile to take their turn at breaking down whenever life threatens to flow smoothly for their human enemies.

Many inanimate objects, of course, find it extremely difficult to break down. Pliers, for example, and gloves and keys are almost totally incapable of breaking down. Therefore, they have had to evolve a different technique for resisting man.

They get lost. Science has still not solved the mystery of how they do it, and no man has ever caught one of them in the act of getting lost. The most plausible theory is that they have developed a secret method of locomotion which they are able to conceal the instant a human eye falls upon them.

It is not uncommon for a pair of pliers to climb all the way from the cellar to the attic in its single-minded determination to raise its owner's blood pressure. Keys have been known to burrow three feet under mattresses. Women's purses, despite their great weight, frequently travel through six or seven rooms to find hiding space under a couch.

Scientists have been struck by the fact that things that break down virtually never get lost, while things that get lost hardly ever break down.

A furnace, for example, will invariably break down at the depth of the first winter cold wave, but it will never get lost. A woman's purse, which after all does have some inherent capacity for breaking down, hardly ever does; it almost invariably chooses to get lost.

Some persons believe this constitutes evidence that inanimate objects are not entirely hostile to man, and that a negotiated peace is possible. After all, they point out, a furnace could infuriate a man even more thoroughly by getting lost than by breaking down, just as a glove could upset him far more by breaking down than by getting lost.

Not everyone agrees, however, that this indicates a conciliatory attitude among inanimate objects. Many say it merely proves that furnaces, gloves, and pliers are incredibly stupid.

The third class of objects—those that don't work—is the most curious of all. These include such objects as barometers, car clocks, cigarette lighters, flashlights, and toy-train locomotives. It is inaccurate, of course, to say that they never work. They work once, usually for the first few hours after being brought home, and then quit. Thereafter, they never work again.

In fact, it is widely assumed that they are built for the purpose of not working. Some people have reached advanced ages without ever seeing some of these objects—barometers, for example—in working order.

Science is utterly baffled by the entire category. There are many theories about it. The most interesting holds that the things that don't work have attained the highest state possible for an inanimate object, the state to which things that break down and things that get lost can still only aspire.

They have truly defeated man by conditioning him never to expect anything of them, and in return they have given man the only peace he receives from inanimate society. He does not expect his barometer to work, his electric locomotive to run, his cigarette lighter to light, or his flashlight to illuminate, and when they don't it does not raise his blood pressure.

He cannot attain that peace with furnaces and keys, and cars and women's purses as long as he demands that they work for their keep.

JOHN CIARDI

Is Everybody Happy?

Called "Mr. Poet" by the *Chicago Tribune*, John Ciardi (1916–1986), born in Boston to Italian immigrants, "propelled poetry into a popular, lively art." After completing his education (M.A., University of Michigan, 1939), Ciardi served as an air force gunner in World War II. As *Saturday Review* poetry editor (1956–1972) and columnist, and through frequent lectures, poetry readings, and television appearances, Ciardi exposed a large audience to poetry. His own award-winning poetry, criticism, and scholarly work include very successful poetry for children (*I Met a Man*, 1969) and a translation of Dante's *Divine Comedy*. In "Is Everybody Happy?", originally published in the *Saturday Review* (1964) and included in *Manner of Speaking* (1972), Ciardi contrasts his definition of happiness with American capitalism's model of "buying our way to happiness." He concludes that "whatever else happiness may be, it is neither in having nor in being, but in becoming." Quoting Robert Frost's praise of "the pleasure of taking pains," Ciardi implies that poetry brings happiness because it is a "life-engaging difficulty." In remarks in the *Writer*, he confirms that "writing poetry is better than easy, it is joyously, consumingly difficult."

The right to pursue happiness is issued to Americans with their birth certificates, but no one seems quite sure which way it ran. It may be we are issued a hunting license but offered no game. Jonathan Swift seemed to think so when he attacked the idea of happiness as "the possession of being well-deceived," the felicity of being "a fool among knaves." For Swift saw society as Vanity Fair, the land of false goals.

It is, of course, un-American to think in terms of fools and knaves. We do, however, seem to be dedicated to the idea of buying our way to happiness. We shall all have made it to Heaven when we possess enough.

And at the same time the forces of American commercialism are hugely dedicated to making us deliberately unhappy. Advertising is one of our major industries, and advertising exists not to satisfy desires but to create them—and to create them faster than any man's budget can satisfy

---

John Ciardi, "Is Everybody Happy?" from *The Saturday Review*, March 14, 1964. By permission of the Ciardi Family Publishing Trust, John L. Ciardi, Trustee.

them. For that matter, our whole economy is based on a dedicated insatiability. We are taught that to possess is to be happy, and then we are made to want. We are even told it is our duty to want. It was only a few years ago, to cite a single example, that car dealers across the country were flying banners that read "You Auto Buy Now." They were calling upon Americans, as an act approaching patriotism, to buy at once, with money they did not have, automobiles they did not really need, and which they would be required to grow tired of by the time the next year's models were released.

Or look at any of the women's magazines. There, as Bernard DeVoto once pointed out, advertising begins as poetry in the front pages and ends as pharmacopoeia and therapy in the back pages. The poetry of the front matter is the dream of perfect beauty. This is the baby skin that must be hers. These, the flawless teeth. This, the perfumed breath she must exhale. This, the sixteen-year-old figure she must display at forty, at fifty, at sixty, and forever.

Once past the vaguely uplifting fiction and feature articles, the reader finds the other face of the dream in the back matter. This is the harness into which Mother must strap herself in order to display that perfect figure. These, the chin straps she must sleep in. This is the salve that restores all, this is her laxative, these are the tablets that melt away fat, these are the hormones of perpetual youth, these are the stockings that hide varicose veins.

Obviously no half-sane person can be completely persuaded either by such poetry or by such pharmacopoeia and orthopedics. Yet someone is obviously trying to buy the dream as offered and spending billions every year in the attempt. Clearly the happiness market is not running out of customers, but what are we trying to buy?

The idea "happiness," to be sure, will not sit still for easy definition: the best one can do is to try to set some extremes to the idea and then work in toward the middle. To think of happiness as acquisitive and competitive will do to set the materialistic extreme. To think of it as the idea one senses in, say, a holy man of India will do to set the spiritual extreme. That holy man's ideal of happiness is in needing nothing from outside himself. In wanting nothing, he lacks nothing. He sits immobile, rapt in contemplation, free even of his own body. Or nearly free of it. If devout admirers bring him food he eats it; if not, he starves indifferently. Why be concerned? What is physical is an illusion to him. Contemplation is his joy and he achieves it through a fantastically demanding discipline, the accomplishment of which is itself a joy within him.

Is he a happy man? Perhaps his happiness is only another sort of illusion. But who can take it from him? And who will dare say it is more illusory than happiness on the installment plan?

But, perhaps because I am Western, I doubt such catatonic happiness, as I doubt the dreams of the happiness market. What is certain is that his way of happiness would be torture to almost any Western man. Yet these extremes will still serve to frame the area within which all of us must find some sort of balance. Thoreau—a creature of both Eastern and Western thought—had his own firm sense of that balance. His aim was to save on the low levels in order to spend on the high.

Possession for its own sake or in competition with the rest of the neighborhood would have been Thoreau's idea of the low levels. The active discipline of heightening one's perception of what is enduring in nature would have been his idea of the high. What he saved from the low was time and effort he could spend on the high. Thoreau certainly disapproved of starvation, but he would put into feeding himself only as much effort as would keep him functioning for more important efforts.

Effort is the gist of it. There is no happiness except as we take on life-engaging difficulties. Short of the impossible, as Yeats put it, the satisfactions we get from a lifetime depend on how high we choose our difficulties. Robert Frost was thinking in something like the same terms when he spoke of "the pleasure of taking pains." The mortal flaw in the advertised version of happiness is in the fact that it purports to be effortless.

We demand difficulty even in our games. We demand it because without difficulty there can be no game. A game is a way of making something hard for the fun of it. The rules of the game are an arbitrary imposition of difficulty. When the spoilsport ruins the fun, he always does so by refusing to play by the rules. It is easier to win at chess if you are free, at your pleasure, to change the wholly arbitrary rules, but the fun is in winning within the rules. No difficulty, no fun.

The buyers and sellers at the happiness market seem too often to have lost their sense of the pleasure of difficulty. Heaven knows what they are playing, but it seems a dull game. The Indian holy man seems dull to us, I suppose, because he seems to be refusing to play anything at all. The Western weakness may be in the illusion that happiness can be bought. Perhaps the Eastern weakness is in the idea that there is such a thing as perfect (and therefore static) happiness.

Happiness is never more than partial. There are no pure states of mankind. Whatever else happiness may be, it is neither in having nor in being, but in becoming. What the Founding Fathers declared for us as an inherent right, we should do well to remember, was not happiness but the *pursuit* of happiness. What they might have underlined, could they have foreseen the happiness market, is the cardinal fact that happiness is in the pursuit itself, in the meaningful pursuit of what is life-engaging and life-revealing, which is to say, in the idea of *becoming*. A nation is not measured by what it possesses or wants to possess, but by what it wants to become.

By all means let the happiness market sell us minor satisfactions and even minor follies so long as we keep them in scale and buy them out of spiritual change. I am no customer for either puritanism or asceticism. But drop any real spiritual capital at those bazaars, and what you come home to will be your own poorhouse.

ESTHER DYSON

Cyberspace for All

Esther Dyson, economist and computer visionary, was named one of the fifty most powerful women in American business by *Fortune* magazine in 1998. Born in Switzerland in 1951 and raised in Princeton, New Jersey, she is the daughter of noted physicist Freeman Dyson and Esther Dyson, a mathematician. At sixteen she entered Harvard, earning a degree in economics in 1972. She has worked for *Forbes*, as a security analyst on Wall Street, and as co-chair of the National Information Infrastructure Advisory Council, Information Privacy and Intellectual Property Subcommittee (1994–1996). She has published two books, *Release 2.0: A Design for Living in the Digital Age* (1997) and *Release 2.1*, an "upgrade" of *Release 2.0*, and she contributes articles to the *New York Times*, the *Harvard Business Review*, and *Wired*. Derek Bickerton, in his review of *Release 2.0*, notes that one of Dyson's goals "is to demystify the Net and thus disarm those who would demonize it." In "Cyberspace for All" (first published in the *New York Times Magazine*, 1995) Dyson persuasively argues against regulation of the Internet, claiming that "regardless of how many laws or lawsuits are launched, regulation won't work." Instead of relying on governmental regulation of cyberspace, Dyson claims that "individual choice—and individual responsibility" are necessary.

Something in the American psyche loves new frontiers. We hanker after wide-open spaces; we like to explore; we like to make rules instead of follow them. But in this age of political correctness and other intrusions on our national cult of independence, it's hard to find a place where you can go and be yourself without worrying about the neighbors.

There is such a place: cyberspace. Lost in the furor over porn on the Net is the exhilarating sense of freedom that this new frontier once promised—and still does in some quarters. Formerly a playground for computer nerds and techies, cyberspace now embraces every conceivable constituency: schoolchildren, flirtatious singles, Hungarian-Americans, accountants—along with pederasts and porn fans. Can they all get along?

Esther Dyson, "Cyberspace for All" from the *New York Times*, July 16, 1995. Copyright © 1995 by The New York Times Co. Reprinted by permission.

Or will our fear of kids surfing for cyberporn behind their bedroom doors provoke a crackdown?

The first order of business is to grasp what cyberspace *is*. It might help to leave behind metaphors of highways and frontiers and to think instead of real estate. Real estate, remember, is an intellectual, legal, artificial environment constructed *on top of* land. Real estate recognizes the difference between parkland and shopping mall, between red light zone and school district, between church, state, and drugstore.

In the same way, you could think of cyberspace as a giant and unbounded world of virtual real estate. Some property is privately owned and rented out; other property is common land; some places are suitable for children, and others are best avoided by all but the kinkiest citizens. Unfortunately, it's those places that are now capturing the popular imagination: places that offer bomb-making instructions, pornography, advice on how to procure stolen credit cards. They make cyberspace sound like a nasty place. Good citizens jump to a conclusion: better regulate it. . . .

Regardless of how many laws or lawsuits are launched, regulation won't work.

Aside from being unconstitutional, using censorship to counter indecency and other troubling "speech" fundamentally misinterprets the nature of cyberspace. Cyberspace isn't a frontier where wicked people can grab unsuspecting children, nor is it a giant television system that can beam offensive messages at unwilling viewers. In this kind of real estate, users have to *choose* where they visit, what they see, what they do. It's optional, and it's much easier to bypass a place on the Net than it is to avoid walking past an unsavory block of stores on the way to your local 7-11.

Put plainly, cyberspace is a voluntary destination—in reality, many destinations. You don't just get "onto the Net"; you have to go someplace in particular. That means that people can choose where to go and what to see. Yes, community standards should be enforced, but those standards should be set by cyberspace communities themselves, not by the courts or by politicians in Washington. What we need isn't Government control over all these electronic communities: We need self-rule.

What makes cyberspace so alluring is precisely the way in which it's *different* from shopping malls, television, highways and other terrestrial jurisdictions. But let's define the territory:

First, there are private e-mail conversations, akin to the conversations you have over the telephone or voice mail. These are private and consensual and require no regulation at all.

Second, there are information and entertainment services, where people can download anything from legal texts and lists of "great new restaurants" to game software or dirty pictures. These places are like bookstores, malls, and movie houses—places where you go to buy something. The customer needs to request an item or sign up for a subscription; stuff (especially pornography) is not sent out to people who don't ask for it. Some of these services are free or included as part of a broad service like Compuserve or America Online; others charge and may bill their customers directly.

Third, there are "real" communities—groups of people who communicate among themselves. In real-estate terms, they're like bars or restaurants or bathhouses. Each active participant contributes to a general conversation, generally through posted messages. Other participants may simply listen or watch. Some are supervised by a moderator; others are more like bulletin boards—anyone is free to post anything. Many of these services started out unmoderated but are now imposing rules to keep out unwanted advertising, extraneous discussions, or increasingly rude participants. Without a moderator, the decibel level often gets too high.

Ultimately, it's the rules that determine the success of such places. Some of the rules are determined by the supplier of content; some of the rules concern prices and membership fees. The rules may be simple: "Only high-quality content about oil-industry liability and pollution legislation: $120 an hour." Or: "This forum is unmoderated, and restricted to information about copyright issues. People who insist on posting advertising or unrelated material will be asked to desist (and may eventually be barred)." Or: "Only children 8 to 12, on school-related topics and only clean words. The moderator will decide what's acceptable."

Cyberspace communities evolve just the way terrestrial communities do: People with like-minded interests band together. Every cyberspace community has its own character. Overall, the communities on Compuserve tend to be more techy or professional; those on America Online, affluent young singles; Prodigy, family oriented. Then there are independents like Echo, a hip, downtown New York service, or Women's Wire, targeted to women who want to avoid the male culture prevalent elsewhere on the Net. There's SurfWatch, a new program allowing access only to locations deemed suitable for children. On the Internet itself, there are lots of passionate noncommercial discussion groups on topics ranging from Hungarian politics (Hungary-Online) to copyright law.

And yes, there are also porn-oriented services, where people share dirty pictures and communicate with one another about all kinds of practices, often anonymously. Whether these services encourage the fantasies they depict is subject to debate—the same debate that has raged about pornography in other media. But the point is that no one is forcing this stuff on anybody.

What's unique about cyberspace is that it liberates us from the tyranny of government, where everyone lives by the rule of the majority. In a democracy, minority groups and minority preferences tend to get squeezed out, whether they are minorities of race and culture or minorities of individual taste. Cyberspace allows communities of any size and kind to flourish; in cyberspace, communities are chosen by the users, not forced on them by accidents of geography. This freedom gives the rules that preside in cyberspace a moral authority that rules in terrestrial environments don't have. Most people are stuck in the country of their birth, but if you don't like the rules of a cyberspace community, you can just sign off. Love it or leave it. Likewise, if parents don't like the rules of a given cyberspace community, they can restrict their children's access to it.

What's likely to happen in cyberspace is the formation of new communities, free of the constraints that cause conflict on earth. Instead of a global village, which is a nice dream but impossible to manage, we'll have invented another world of self-contained communities that cater to their own members' inclinations without interfering with anyone else's. The possibility of a real market-style evolution of governance is at hand. In cyberspace, we'll be able to test and evolve rules governing what needs to be governed—intellectual property, content and access control, rules about privacy and free speech. Some communities will allow anyone in; others will restrict access to members who qualify on one basis or another. Those communities that prove self-sustaining will prosper (and perhaps grow and split into subsets with ever-more-particular interests and identities). Those that can't survive—either because people lose interest or get scared off—will simply wither away.

In the near future, explorers in cyberspace will need to get better at defining and identifying their communities. They will need to put in place—and accept—their own local governments, just as the owners of expensive real estate often prefer to have their own security guards rather than call in the police. But they will rarely need help from any terrestrial government.

Of course, terrestrial governments may not agree. What to do, for instance, about pornography? The answer is labeling—not banning— questionable material. In order to avoid censorship and lower the political temperature, it makes sense for cyberspace participants themselves to agree on a scheme for questionable items, so that people or automatic filters can avoid them. In other words, posting pornography in "alt.sex.bestiality" would be O.K.; it's easy enough for software manufacturers to build an automatic filter that would prevent you—or your child—from ever seeing that item on a menu. (It's as if all the items were wrapped, with labels on the wrapper.) Someone who posted the same material under the title "Kid-Fun" could be sued for mislabeling.

Without a lot of fanfare, private enterprises and local groups are already producing a variety of labeling and ranking services, along with kid-oriented sites like Kidlink, EdWeb and Kids' Space. People differ in their tastes and values and can find services or reviewers on the Net that suit them in the same way they select books and magazines. Or they can wander freely if they prefer, making up their own itinerary.

In the end, our society needs to grow up. Growing up means understanding that there are no perfect answers, no all-purpose solutions, no government-sanctioned safe havens. We haven't created a perfect society on earth and we won't have one in cyberspace either. But at least we can have individual choice—and individual responsibility.

BARBARA EHRENREICH

Oh, Those *Family Values*

Journalist Barbara Ehrenreich, born in Butte, Montana (1941), and educated at Reed College and Rockefeller University (Ph.D., biology, 1968), contributes to many national magazines, including *The Progressive*, *Time* magazine, and *Harper's*. She writes about social justice and women's issues, often from personal or humorous perspectives. She began her career using her scientific training to write about health care and has written (often collaboratively) a number of books on feminist and class issues, including the controversial *The Hearts of Men* (1983), which argues that it is not feminism, but men's "flight from commitment," that has weakened families. Critics praise her as witty and provocative even when they fault her analysis; Laura Shapiro in *Newsweek* (1987) admires her "left-wing political convictions, unfashionable but unflinching, tempered only by good humor." In "Oh, *Those* Family Values," published in *Time* (1994) and collected in *The Snarling Citizen* (1995), Ehrenreich analyzes what she has described as "our contemporary zeitgeist . . . a low, snarly creature that oozes out from the TV and settles lumplike into the den." She cites events culled from "zeitgeist-watching" to show that, far from being sanctified havens of peace and goodness, families are often "the most dangerous place to be."

A disturbing subtext runs through our recent media fixations. Parents abuse sons—allegedly at least, in the Menendez case—who in turn rise up and kill them. A husband torments a wife, who retaliates with a kitchen knife. Love turns into obsession, between the Simpsons anyway, and then perhaps into murderous rage: the family, in other words, becomes personal hell.

This accounts for at least part of our fascination with the Bobbitts and the Simpsons and the rest of them. We live in a culture that fetishes the family as the ideal unit of human community, the perfect container for our lusts and loves. Politicians of both parties are aggressively "pro-family," even abortion-rights bumper stickers proudly link "pro-family" and "pro-choice." Only with the occasional celebrity crime do we allow ourselves to think the nearly unthinkable: that the family may not be the ideal and perfect living arrangement after all—that it can be a nest of pathology and a cradle of gruesome violence.

It's a scary thought, because the family is at the same time our "haven in a heartless world." Theoretically, and sometimes actually, the family nurtures warm, loving feelings, uncontaminated by greed or power hunger. Within the family, and often only within the family, individuals are loved "for themselves," whether or not they are infirm, incontinent, infantile, or eccentric. The strong (adults and especially males) lie down peaceably with the small and weak.

But consider the matter of wife battery. We managed to dodge it in the Bobbitt case and downplay it as a force in Tonya Harding's life. Thanks to O. J., though, we're caught up now in a mass consciousness-raising session, grimly absorbing the fact that in some areas domestic violence sends as many women to emergency rooms as any other form of illness, injury, or assault.

Still, we shrink from the obvious inference: For a woman, home is, statistically speaking, the most dangerous place to be. Her worst enemies and potential killers are not strangers but lovers, husbands, and those who claimed to love her once. Similarly, for every child like Polly Klaas who is killed by a deranged criminal on parole, dozens are abused and murdered by their own relatives. Home is all too often where the small and weak fear to lie down and shut their eyes.

At some deep, queasy, Freudian level, we all know this. Even in the ostensibly "functional," nonviolent family, where no one is killed or maimed, feelings are routinely bruised and often twisted out of shape. There is the slap or put-down that violates a child's shaky sense of self, the cold, distracted stare that drives a spouse to tears, the little digs and rivalries. At best, the family teaches the finest things human beings can learn from one another—generosity and love. But it is also, all too often, where we learn nasty things like hate and rage and shame.

Americans act out their ambivalence about the family without ever owning up to it. Millions adhere to creeds that are militantly "pro-family." But at the same time millions flock to therapy groups that offer to heal the "inner child" from damage inflicted by family life. Legions of women band together to revive the self-esteem they lost in supposedly loving relationships and to learn to love a little less. We are all, it is often said, "in recovery." And from what? Our families, in most cases.

There is a long and honorable tradition of "anti-family" thought. The French philosopher Charles Fourier taught that the family was a barrier to human progress; early feminists saw a degrading parallel between marriage and prostitution. More recently, the renowned British anthropologist

Edmund Leach stated that "far from being the basis of the good society, the family, with its narrow privacy and tawdry secrets, is the source of all discontents."

Communes proved harder to sustain than plain old couples, and the conservatism of the eighties crushed the last vestiges of life-style experimentation. Today even gays and lesbians are eager to get married and take up family life. Feminists have learned to couch their concerns as "family issues," and public figures would sooner advocate free cocaine on demand than criticize the family. Hence our unseemly interest in O. J. and Erik, Lyle, and Lorena: they allow us, however gingerly, to break the silence on the hellish side of family life.

But the discussion needs to become a lot more open and forthright. We may be stuck with the family—at least until someone invents a sustainable alternative—but the family, with its deep, impacted tensions and longings, can hardly be expected to be the moral foundation of everything else. In fact, many families could use a lot more outside interference in the form of counseling and policing, and some are so dangerously dysfunctional that they ought to be encouraged to disband right away. Even healthy families need outside sources of moral guidance to keep the internal tensions from imploding—and this means, at the very least, a public philosophy of gender equality and concern for child welfare. When, instead, the larger culture aggrandizes wife beaters, degrades women or nods approvingly at child slappers, the family gets a little more dangerous for everyone, and so, inevitably, does the larger world.

WILLIAM FAULKNER

Nobel Prize Award Speech

Almost all of William Faulkner's fiction focuses on Mississippi, his birthplace, and the site of his fictional world, Yoknapatawpha County. Faulkner (1897–1962) never finished high school but read widely on his own. With his regional focus and experimental narrative techniques in such novels as *The Sound and the Fury* (1929), *As I Lay Dying* (1930), *Light in August* (1932), and *Absalom, Absalom!* (1936), Faulkner created masterpieces exploring the conflicts within the human heart. His modernist style, his syntactically complex sentences, and his focus on racial issues and on subjects sensational in their day impeded Faulkner's achieving literary success for many years. Faulkner spent several short stints as a Hollywood scriptwriter of such films as *To Have and Have Not* (1945) and *The Big Sleep* (1946). The publication of *The Portable Faulkner* (1946), edited by Malcolm Cowley, rehabilitated his reputation. The Nobel Prize, conferred on Faulkner following the publication of his antiracist novel *Intruder in the Dust* (1948), confirmed his status as a major figure in world literature. In his acceptance speech for the prize (1950), Faulkner responds to the imminent nuclear threat of the Cold War: humanity is immortal, because mankind "has a soul, a spirit capable of compassion and sacrifice and endurance."

I feel that this award was not made to me as a man but to my work—a life's work in the agony and sweat of the human spirit, not for glory and least of all for profit, but to create out of the materials of the human spirit something which did not exist before. So this award is only mine in trust. It will not be difficult to find a dedication for the money part of it commensurate with the purpose and significance of its origin. But I would like to do the same with the acclaim too, by using this moment as a pinnacle from which I might be listened to by the young men and women already dedicated to the same anguish and travail, among whom is already that one who will some day stand here where I am standing.

Our tragedy today is a general and universal physical fear so long sustained by now that we can even bear it. There are no longer problems of the spirit. There is only the question: When will I be blown up? Because of this, the young man or woman writing today has forgotten the problems of the human heart in conflict with itself which alone can make good writing because only that is worth writing about, worth the agony and the sweat.

He must learn them again. He must teach himself that the basest of all things is to be afraid; and, teaching himself that, forget it forever, leaving no room in his workshop for anything but the old verities and truths of the heart, the old universal truths lacking which any story is ephemeral and doomed—love and honor and pity and pride and compassion and sacrifice. Until he does so, he labors under a curse. He writes not of love but of lust, of defeats in which nobody loses anything of value, of victories without hope and, worst of all, without pity or compassion. His griefs grieve on no universal bones, leaving no scars. He writes not of the heart but of the glands.

Until he relearns these things, he will write as though he stood alone and watched the end of man. I decline to accept the end of man. It is easy enough to say that man is immortal simply because he will endure; that when the last ding-dong of doom has clanged and faded from the last worthless rock hanging tideless in the last red and dying evening, that even then there will still be one more sound: that of his puny inexhaustible voice, still talking. I refuse to accept this. I believe that man will not merely endure: he will prevail. He is immortal, not because he alone among creatures has an inexhaustible voice but because he has a soul, a spirit capable of compassion and sacrifice and endurance. The poet's, the writer's, duty is to write about these things. It is his privilege to help man endure by lifting his heart, by reminding him of the courage and honor and hope and pride and compassion and pity and sacrifice which have been the glory of his past. The poet's voice need not merely be the record of man, it can be one of the props, the pillars to help him endure and prevail.

MILTON FRIEDMAN

Prohibition and Drugs

Economist and Nobel laureate for Economic Science (1976) Milton Friedman (born 1912) earned an A.B. from Rutgers (1932), an A.M. from the University of Chicago (1933), and a Ph.D. from Columbia (1946). As a professor of economics at the University of Chicago (1948–1982), Friedman was the leader of the Chicago School of Economics, a group of likeminded economists who called for an end to government intervention in all aspects of the economy. Friedman's conservative fiscal policies were particularly influential during the Reagan presidency. Friedman has outlined his basic belief that less is more when it comes to government in numerous books, from *Essays in Positive Economics* (1953) to *Tax Limitation, Inflation, and the Role of Government* (1979) and *Foreign Economic Aid: Means and Objectives* (1995). In "Prohibition and Drugs" (first published in *Newsweek*, 1972) Friedman's argument is twofold. First he argues against the prohibition of drugs, claiming that "Prohibition is an attempted cure that makes matters worse—for both the addict and the rest of us," and then for the legalization of drugs as a means of "reduc[ing] the amount of crime and rais[ing] the quality of law enforcement."

"The reign of tears is over. The slums will soon be only a memory. We will turn our prisons into factories and our jails into storehouses and corncribs. Men will walk upright now, women will smile, and the children will laugh. Hell will be forever for rent."

That is how Billy Sunday, the noted evangelist and leading crusader against Demon Rum, greeted the onset of Prohibition in early 1920. We know now how tragically his hopes were doomed. New prisons and jails had to be built to house the criminals spawned by converting the drinking of spirits into a crime against the state. Prohibition undermined respect for the law, corrupted the minions of the law, created a decadent moral climate—but did not stop the consumption of alcohol.

Despite this tragic object lesson, we seem bent on repeating precisely the same mistake in the handling of drugs.

Milton Friedman, "Prohibition and Drugs" from *Newsweek*, May 1, 1972. Copyright © 1972 Newsweek, Inc. All rights reserved. Reprinted by permission.

Ethics and Expediency

On ethical grounds, do we have the right to use the machinery of government to prevent an individual from becoming an alcoholic or a drug addict? For children, almost everyone would answer at least a qualified yes. But for responsible adults, I, for one, would answer no. Reason with the potential addict, yes. Tell him the consequences, yes. Pray for and with him, yes. But I believe that we have no right to use force, directly or indirectly, to prevent a fellow man from committing suicide, let alone from drinking alcohol or taking drugs.

I readily grant that the ethical issue is difficult and that men of goodwill may well disagree. Fortunately, we need not resolve the ethical issue to agree on policy. *Prohibition is an attempted cure that makes matters worse—for both the addict and the rest of us.* Hence, even if you regard present policy toward drugs as ethically justified, considerations of expediency make that policy most unwise.

Consider first the addict. Legalizing drugs might increase the number of addicts, but it is not clear that it would. Forbidden fruit is attractive, particularly to the young. More important, many drug addicts are deliberately made by pushers, who give likely prospects their first few doses free. It pays the pusher to do so because, once hooked, the addict is a captive customer. If drugs were legally available, any possible profit from such inhumane activity would disappear, since the addict could buy from the cheapest source.

Whatever happens to the number of addicts, the individual addict would clearly be far better off if drugs were legal. Today, drugs are both incredibly expensive and highly uncertain in quality. Addicts are driven to associate with criminals to get the drugs, become criminals themselves to finance the habit, and risk constant danger of death and disease.

Consider next the rest of us. Here the situation is crystal-clear. The harm to us from the addiction of others arises almost wholly from the fact that drugs are illegal. A recent committee of the American Bar Association estimated that addicts commit one-third to one-half of all street crime in the U.S. Legalize drugs, and street crime would drop dramatically.

Moreover, addicts and pushers are not the only ones corrupted. Immense sums are at stake. It is inevitable that some relatively low-paid police and other government officials—and some high-paid ones as well—will succumb to the temptation to pick up easy money.

Law and Order

Legalizing drugs would simultaneously reduce the amount of crime and raise the quality of law enforcement. Can you conceive of any other measure that would accomplish so much to promote law and order?

But, you may say, must we accept defeat? Why not simply end the drug traffic? That is where experience under Prohibition is most relevant. We cannot end the drug traffic. We may be able to cut off opium from Turkey—but there are innumerable other places where the opium poppy grows. With French cooperation, we may be able to make Marseilles an unhealthy place to manufacture heroin—but there are innumerable other places where the simple manufacturing operations involved can be carried out. So long as large sums of money are involved—and they are bound to be if drugs are illegal—it is literally hopeless to expect to end the traffic or even to reduce seriously its scope.

In drugs, as in other areas, persuasion and example are likely to be far more effective than the use of force to shape others in our image.

PETE HAMILL

Winning Isn't Everything

Pete Hamill (born 1935) is an award-winning reporter (*Newsday*, *New York Daily News*), columnist (*Village Voice*, *Esquire*), fiction writer (*Flesh and Blood*, 1977; *Snow in August*, 1997), autobiographer (*A Drinking Life*, 1994), and writer of screenplays (*Nightside*, 1973; *Liberty*, 1986). He quit school at age sixteen to help support his large Irish American family; after he served in the navy, aid from the G.I. Bill helped him to attend the Pratt Institute (1955 and 1958), after which he studied art for a year at Mexico City College (now University of the Americas). In "Winning Isn't Everything" (originally published in *Gentleman's Quarterly*, 1983), Hamill argues against the view of Vince Lombardi, legendary coach of the Green Bay Packers, who said, "Winning isn't everything, it's the only thing." In politics, business, and other significant human relationships, the ethos of Humphrey Bogart, courageous and compassionate, has given way to that of John Wayne, "the swaggering macho blowhard." But according to Hamill, we learn as much from defeat as from victory, which are "inseparable brothers."

One of the more widely accepted maxims of modern American life was uttered on a frozen winter afternoon during the early sixties. The late Vince Lombardi, who coached the Green Bay Packers when they were the greatest team in football, said it. "Winning isn't everything," he declared. "It's the only thing."

Vince Lombardi's notion was immediately appropriated by an extraordinary variety of American males: presidents and lesser politicians, generals, broadcasters, political columnists, Little League coaches, heads of corporations, and probably millions of others. In fact, it sometimes seems that Lombardi's words have had greater impact than any sentence uttered by an American since Stephen Decatur's "our country, right or wrong."

That's surprising on many levels, beginning with the obvious: It's a deceptively simple premise. Winning *isn't* "the only thing." Such an idea muddles the idea of competition, not simply in sports, but in all aspects of our lives. We've learned the hard way in this century that the world is a complex place; it's certainly not the National Football League. Winning

---

Pete Hamill, "Winning Isn't Everything" copyright © 1983 by Pete Hamill. From *Gentleman's Quarterly*, 1983. Reprinted by permission of International Creative Management, Inc.

isn't the only thing in love, art, marriage, commerce, or politics; it's not even the only thing in sports.

In sports, as in so many other areas of our national life, we've always cherished gallant losers. I remember one afternoon in the fall of 1956 when Sal Maglie was pitching for the Brooklyn Dodgers against the hated Yankees. Maglie was an old man that year, as age is measured in sports. But this was the World Series, and he hauled his thirty-nine-year-old body to the mound, inning after inning, gave everything he had, held the Yankees to a few scattered hits and two runs—and lost. That day Don Larsen pitched his perfect game: no runs, no hits, no errors. Yet, to me, the afternoon belong to Maglie—tough, gallant, and a loser.

There was an evening in Manila when Joe Frazier went up against Muhammad Ali for the third and final time. That night, Frazier brought his workman's skills into combat against the magic of the artist, called on his vast reservoir of courage and will, and came up empty at the end of fourteen rounds. Frazier was the loser, but that evening, nobody really lost. Because of that fight, Joe Frazier can always boast with honor that he made Muhammad Ali a great fighter. He was the test, the implacable force who made Ali summon all of his own considerable reserves of skill, heart, and endurance for a final effort. The contest consumed them both. Neither was ever again a good fighter. But during their violent confrontation, winning or losing was, in the end, a marginal concern; that all-consuming effort was everything.

There are hundreds of similar examples of losers who showed us how to be more human, and their performances make the wide acceptance of Lombardi's notions even more mystifying. Lombardi's thesis, in fact, represented something of a shift in the nation's popular thought. Americans had been the people who remembered the Alamo or Pearl Harbor; we blew taps over the graves of those who lost at the Battle of the Bulge or Anzio or the Yalu Basin. Those soldiers had all been defeated, but we honored them for their display of a critical human quality: courage.

Ernest Hemingway once defined courage as grace under pressure, and that's always struck me as an eminently useful definition. The best professional athletes not only possess that kind of courage but, more important, are willing to display it to strangers. Baseball's Reggie Jackson or Richard ("Goose") Gossage, for instance, function most completely as athletes and as men when appearing before gigantic crowds under pressure: bases loaded, late innings, a big game. They come to their tasks with gladness and absolute focus, neither whimpering, complaining, nor shirking when doing their job; they just try their best to get that job done. And, of course, sometimes they fail. Gossage gives up a single and his team loses. Jackson strikes out. No matter. The important thing is that such men keep their appointments with confidence and grace. Courage has become so deep a part of their character that they don't even think about it. (They certainly *want* to win. Sometimes they absolutely lust for victory. But they know that winning isn't everything. All a man can do is his best.)

Competition isn't really a problem for Americans. All sports, in one way or another, are competitive. But an individual's primary competition is with himself and all his attendant weaknesses. That's obviously true of boxing, where fear must be dominated and made to work to the fighter's benefit. Yet it's also true for team sports, as well as such solitary endeavors as golf, where a player must learn control before anything else. The problem isn't competition, which is a part of life; it's in the notion of the necessity of triumph. A man can lose but still win. And the point of competition in sports is an old and not very fashionable one: It builds character.

That's especially true of prizefighters, the athletes I've known best. Outside the ring, almost all fighters are the gentlest of men. They carry themselves with the dignity of those who have little to prove, either to others or themselves. They're not bullies, rarely use their dangerous skills against ordinary citizens and avoid pointless confrontations. When a fighter hears that a colleague has been involved in a bar brawl or a swingout with a cop, he dismisses that fighter as a cowardly bum. Most of the boxers I know are honest, generous, funny. Yet they also know that as good as they are, there might be someone down the line who has their number. Again, they would prefer to be winners. But they're aware that losing, if a courageous effort is made, is never a disgrace. The highest compliment one fighter can pay another is to say that he has "heart."

There are lessons to be learned from such athletes that can be applied to how we live our lives. In the long run, we'll all come up losers because there's no greater loss than death. And since primitive man first began to think, we humans have devised strategies to deal with dying. Religion is the most obvious one, usually demanding that we adhere to a moral code on earth in exchange for a serene existence after death. Ideologies offer secular versions of the same instinct, insisting that we sacrifice now, directing our lives toward the ideal of a better future, with each man becoming an architect of his own utopia. Patriotism and nationalism carry some of the same fearful baggage.

An athlete's goals are less cosmic, his field of struggle less grandiose and therefore more applicable to ordinary citizens. Great athletes teach us that life is a series of struggles, not one giant effort. Just when we appear to have triumphed, we must stop like Sisyphus and again begin rolling the boulder up that mountain. The true athlete teaches us that winning isn't everything, but struggle is—the struggle to simply get up in the morning or to see hope through the minefields of despair.

Viewed that way, a marriage, or any relationship with another human being, is an ongoing struggle. The mastering of a skill or craft doesn't end with the granting of a diploma; it goes on for life. The relationship between parents and children doesn't end when the children turn eighteen. The running of a corporation isn't a one-shot affair, measured by a single year's statements of profits and losses; it's a continuing process, accomplished by human beings who learn from mistakes, plunge fearlessly into the struggle, take risks, and prepare for the future.

It's probably no accident that American capitalism, with its often permanently infantile male executives, experienced a decline that coincided with the period when Vince Lombardi's values received their widest acceptance. The results are visible everywhere. Sit on a plane with American businessmen and they'll be chattering about the Pittsburgh Steelers. Join a group of Japanese businessmen and they'll be discussing twenty-first-century technology. One group is trapped in a philosophy that demands winning as its goal; the other cares more about patient, long-term growth—and for the moment at least, the latter is winning.

Another great maxim of the years of America's triumphs also came from the sports page via the writer Grantland Rice: "It matters not who won or lost," declared the esteemed chronicler of the prewar years, "but how they played the game." By the time Vince Lombardi came along, such sentiments were being sneered at. We had then become a superpower, capable of blowing up the world. The man of grace, courage, endurance, and compassion was replaced in the public imagination by the swaggering macho blowhard; Humphrey Bogart gave way to John Wayne. With such attitudes dominating the landscape, we were certain to get into trouble, and we did. Vietnam and Watergate underscored the idea of winning at all costs. Yet today we seem incapable of admitting that an obsession with winning often leads to the most squalid of defeats.

Solid marriages are often built upon the experience of disastrous ones. Politicians who lose elections become tempered for the contests that follow, sometimes going on to solid, useful careers. Painters, playwrights, novelists, and other artists often learn as much from their failures as they do from those rare moments when vision, craft, and ambition come together to produce masterpieces. It's also that way in sports.

I remember a night when my friend José Torres, then a middleweight, was boxing Florentino Fernandez in Puerto Rico. I couldn't go to the fight, so I spent the night tuning in and out of the all-news radio stations, anxious about the result because Florentino was a great puncher. About three in the morning, Torres called.

"Oh, Pete," he said, close to tears. "I'm so sorry."

"What happened?"

"I got knocked out," Torres replied, his voice brimming with emotion, since he'd never lost as a professional. We started discussing what had happened. Emotions cooled; the talk became technical. Torres explained that he had learned some things about himself, about boxing. He now understood some of his flaws, and thought he could correct them. We talked for an hour. Then I asked what he was going to do next.

"Go to the gym," he said. "I'm going to be champion of the world."

Two years later, Torres *was* the world's light-heavyweight champion. He didn't quit after his first defeat. That night in San Juan he didn't say winning was the only thing, that it was time to pack it in. He had learned something from defeat, and knew that one violent night, somewhere down the line, he would show the world what he had learned. And that was precisely what he did. But he was aware of something else too: Sooner or later, someone might come along who was better than he was, for at least one evening. After all, even champions are human. Even champions eventually lose. That happened to José Torres as well. But then it didn't really matter. José Torres, like the rest of us, had learned that winning wasn't everything. Living was all, and in life, defeat and victory are inseparable brothers.

SUSAN JACOBY

Notes from a Free-Speech Junkie

Susan Jacoby, born in Chicago (1945) and educated at Michigan State University (B.A., 1965), began her journalism career as education reporter for the *Washington Post*. She and her husband, the *Post*'s Moscow correspondent, lived in the Soviet Union (1969–1971), and her experiences are recorded in *Moscow Conversations* (1972), *The Friendship Barrier* (1972), and *Inside Soviet Schools* (1974). In 1979, she published *The Possible She*, a collection of her *New York Times* essays on women. According to R. L. Widman of the *Washington Post*, "her best writing usually features impassioned understanding and descriptions of people," based on interviews and her own experiences. Other books include *Wild Justice: The Evolution of Revenge* (1983) and *Half-Jew* (2000), a personal memoir exploring her hidden Jewish heritage. In "Notes from a Free-Speech Junkie" (1978), a *Times* column, Jacoby disagrees with feminists, such as Margaret Atwood, who advocate controls on pornography. Declaring that she believes in "an absolute interpretation of the First Amendment," which guarantees free speech, Jacoby argues that it is impossible to restrict the more objectionable kinds of pornography without also permitting censorship of any expressions that people find offensive, including discussions of health issues and positive depictions of women's sexual experiences.

It is no news that many women are defecting from the ranks of civil libertarians on the issue of obscenity. The conviction of Larry Flynt, publisher of *Hustler* magazine—before his metamorphosis into a born-again Christian—was greeted with unabashed feminist approval. Harry Reems, the unknown actor who was convicted by a Memphis jury for conspiring to distribute the movie *Deep Throat,* has carried on his legal battles with almost no support from women who ordinarily regard themselves as supporters of the First Amendment. Feminist writers and scholars have even discussed the possibility of making common cause against pornography with adversaries of the women's movement—including opponents of the equal rights amendment and "right to life" forces.

Susan Jacoby, "Notes from a Free-Speech Junkie" from *The Possible She*. Copyright © 1978 by Susan Jacoby. Reprinted by permission of Georges Borchardt, Inc. for the author.

All of this is deeply disturbing to a woman writer who believes, as I always have and still do, in an absolute interpretation of the First Amendment. Nothing in Larry Flynt's garbage convinces me that the late Justice Hugo L. Black was wrong in his opinion that "the federal government is without any power whatsoever under the Constitution to put any type of burden on free speech and expression of ideas of any kind (as distinguished from conduct)." Many women I like and respect tell me I am wrong; I cannot remember having become involved in so many heated discussions of a public issue since the end of the Vietnam War. A feminist writer described my views as those of a "First Amendment junkie."

Many feminist arguments for controls on pornography carry the implicit conviction that porn books, magazines, and movies pose a greater threat to women than similarly repulsive exercises of free speech pose to other offended groups. This conviction has, of course, been shared by everyone—regardless of race, creed, or sex—who has ever argued in favor of abridging the First Amendment. It is the argument used by some Jews who have withdrawn their support from the American Civil Liberties Union because it has defended the right of American Nazis to march through a community inhabited by survivors of Hitler's concentration camps.

If feminists want to argue that the protection of the Constitution should not be extended to *any* particularly odious or threatening form of speech, they have a reasonable argument (although I don't agree with it). But it is ridiculous to suggest that the porn shops on 42nd Street are more disgusting to women than a march of neo-Nazis is to survivors of the extermination camps.

The arguments over pornography also blur the vital distinction between expression of ideas and conduct. When I say I believe unreservedly in the First Amendment, someone always comes back at me with the issue of "kiddie porn." But kiddie porn is not a First Amendment issue. It is an issue of the abuse of power—the power adults have over children—and not of obscenity. Parents and promoters have no more right to use their children to make porn movies than they do to send them to work in coal mines. The responsible adults should be prosecuted, just as adults who use children for back-breaking farm labor should be prosecuted.

Susan Brownmiller, in *Against Our Will: Men, Women, and Rape*, has described pornography as "the undiluted essence of antifemale propaganda." I think this is a fair description of some types of pornography, especially of the brutish subspecies that equates sex with death and portrays women primarily as objects of violence.

The equation of sex and violence, personified by some glossy rock record album covers as well as by *Hustler*, has fed the illusion that censorship of pornography can be conducted on a more rational basis than other types of censorship. Are all pictures of naked women obscene? Clearly not, says a friend. A Renoir nude is art, she says, and *Hustler* is trash. "Any reasonable person" knows that.

But what about something between art and trash—something, say, along the lines of *Playboy* or *Penthouse* magazines? I asked five women for their reactions to one picture in *Penthouse* and got responses that ranged from "lovely" and "sensuous" to "revolting" and "demeaning." Feminists, like everyone else, seldom have rational reasons for their preferences in erotica. Like members of juries, they tend to disagree when confronted with something that falls short of 100 percent vulgarity.

In any case, feminists will not be the arbiters of good taste if it becomes easier to harass, prosecute, and convict people on obscenity charges. Most of the people who want to censor girlie magazines are equally opposed to open discussion of issues that are of vital concern to women: rape, abortion, menstruation, contraception, lesbianism—in fact, the entire range of sexual experience from a woman's viewpoint.

Feminist writers and editors and filmmakers have limited financial resources: Confronted by a determined prosecutor, Hugh Hefner will fare better than Susan Brownmiller. Would the Memphis jurors who convicted Harry Reems for his role in *Deep Throat* be inclined to take a more positive view of paintings of the female genitalia done by sensitive feminist artists? *Ms.* magazine has printed color reproductions of some of those art works; *Ms.* is already banned from a number of high school libraries because someone considers it threatening and/or obscene.

Feminists who want to censor what they regard as harmful pornography have essentially the same motivation as other would-be censors: They want to use the power of the state to accomplish what they have been unable to achieve in the marketplace of ideas and images. The impulse to censor places no faith in the possibilities of democratic persuasion.

It isn't easy to persuade certain men that they have better uses for $1.95 each month than to spend it on a copy of *Hustler*? Well, then, give the men no choice in the matter.

I believe there is also a connection between the impulse toward censorship on the part of people who used to consider themselves civil libertarians and a more general desire to shift responsibility from individuals to institutions. When I saw the movie *Looking for Mr. Goodbar*, I was stunned by its series of visual images equating sex and violence, coupled with what seems to me the mindless message (a distortion of the fine Judith Rossner novel) that casual sex equals death. When I came out of the movie, I was even more shocked to see parents standing in line with children between the ages of ten and fourteen.

I simply don't know why a parent would take a child to see such a movie, any more than I understand why people feel they can't turn off a television set their child is watching. Whenever I say that, my friends tell me I don't know how it is because I don't have children. True, but I do have parents. When I was a child, they did turn off the TV. They didn't expect the Federal Communications Commission to do their job for them.

I am a First Amendment junkie. You can't OD on the First Amendment, because free speech is its own best antidote.

THOMAS JEFFERSON

The Declaration of Independence

Thomas Jefferson (1743–1826), of Charlottesville, Virginia, was—like his fellow patriot Benjamin Franklin—a renaissance man. Educated at the College of William and Mary, later the founder of the University of Virginia, Jefferson excelled as a philosopher, architect, inventor, writer, and, above all, a consummate politician. A patrician and revolutionary who embodied the democratic spirit of the new nation, Jefferson served as a delegate to the Continental Congress in 1775, as governor of the Commonwealth of Virginia, and as third president of the United States. With Franklin and John Adams, Jefferson drafted America's most incendiary document, the Declaration of Independence, in mid-June 1776. Revised by the Continental Congress, it was signed on July 4. The Declaration, often called "an expression of the American mind," reflects Jefferson's belief that democracy is the ideal form of government, a philosophy reinforced in his refusal to sign the Constitution until the Bill of Rights was added. The Declaration is a deductive argument, based on the premise "We hold these truths to be self-evident," from which the rest of the argument follows. As events were to prove, what the colonists considered an emphatic, plainspoken statement of natural rights the British considered an inflammatory declaration of war.

IN CONGRESS, JULY 4, 1776
THE UNANIMOUS DECLARATION OF THE
THIRTEEN UNITED STATES OF AMERICA

When in the Course of human events it becomes necessary for one people to dissolve the political bands which have connected them with another, and to assume among the powers of the earth, the separate and equal station to which the Laws of Nature and of Nature's God entitle them, a decent respect to the opinions of mankind requires that they should declare the causes which impel them to the separation.

We hold these truths to be self-evident, that all men are created equal, that they are endowed by their Creator with certain unalienable Rights, that among these are Life, Liberty, and the pursuit of Happiness. That to secure these rights, Governments are instituted among Men, deriving their just powers from the consent of the governed. That whenever any Form of Government becomes destructive of these ends, it is the Right of the People to alter or to abolish it, and to institute new Government, laying its foundation on such principles and organizing its powers in such form, as to them shall seem most likely to effect their Safety and Happiness. Prudence, indeed, will dictate that Governments long established should not be changed for light and transient causes; and accordingly all experience hath shewn, that mankind are more disposed to suffer, while evils are sufferable, than to right themselves by abolishing the forms to which they are accustomed. But when a long train of abuses and usurpations, pursuing invariably the same Object evinces a design to reduce them under absolute Despotism, it is their right, it is their duty, to throw off such Government, and to provide new Guards for their future security. Such has been the patient sufferance of these Colonies; and such is now the necessity which constrains them to alter their former Systems of Government. The history of the present King of Great Britain is a history of repeated injuries and usurpations, all having in direct object the establishment of an absolute Tyranny over these States. To prove this, let Facts be submitted to a candid world.

He has refused his Assent to Laws, the most wholesome and necessary for the public good.

He has forbidden his Governors to pass laws of immediate and pressing importance, unless suspended in their operation till his Assent should be obtained; and when so suspended, he has utterly neglected to attend to them.

He has refused to pass other Laws for the accommodation of large districts of people, unless those people would relinquish the right of Representation in the Legislature, a right inestimable to them and formidable to tyrants only.

He has called together legislative bodies at places unusual, uncomfortable, and distant from the depository of their Public Records, for the sole purpose of fatiguing them into compliance with his measures.

He has dissolved Representative Houses repeatedly, for opposing with manly firmness his invasions on the rights of the people.

He has refused for a long time, after such dissolutions, to cause others to be elected; whereby the Legislative Powers, incapable of Annihilation, have returned to the People at large for their exercise; the State remaining in the mean time exposed to all the dangers of invasion from without, and convulsions within.

He has endeavoured to prevent the population of these States; for that purpose obstructing the Laws for Naturalization of Foreigners; refusing to pass others to encourage their migration hither, and raising the conditions of new Appropriations of Lands.

He has obstructed the Administration of Justice, by refusing his Assent to Laws for establishing Judiciary Powers.

He has made Judges dependent on his Will alone, for the tenure of their offices, and the amount and payment of their salaries.

He has erected a multitude of New Offices, and sent hither swarms of Officers to harass our People, and eat out their substance.

He has kept among us, in times of peace, Standing Armies without the Consent of our legislatures.

He has affected to render the Military independent of and superior to the Civil Power.

He has combined with others to subject us to a jurisdiction foreign to our constitution, and unacknowledged by our laws; giving his Assent to their Acts of pretended Legislation: For quartering large bodies of armed troops among us: For protecting them, by a mock Trial, from punishment for any Murders which they should commit on the Inhabitants of these States: For cutting off our Trade with all parts of the world: For imposing Taxes on us without our Consent: For depriving us in many cases, of the benefits of Trial by Jury; For transporting us beyond Seas to be tried for pretended offenses: for abolishing the free System of English Laws in a neighboring Province, establishing therein an Arbitrary government, and enlarging its Boundaries so as to render it at once an example and fit instrument for introducing the same absolute rule into these Colonies: For taking away our Charters, abolishing our most valuable Laws and altering fundamentally the Forms of our Governments: For suspending our own Legislatures, and declaring themselves invested with power to legislate for us in all cases whatsoever.

He has abdicated Government here, by declaring us out of his Protection and waging War against us.

He has plundered our seas, ravaged our Coasts, burnt our towns, and destroyed the lives of our people.

He is at this time transporting large Armies of foreign Mercenaries to complete the works of death, desolation and tyranny, already begun with circumstances of Cruelty & Perfidy scarcely paralleled in the most barbarous ages, and totally unworthy the Head of a civilized nation.

He has constrained our fellow Citizens taken Captive on the high Seas to bear Arms against their Country, to become the executioners of their friends and Brethren, or to fall themselves by their Hands.

He has excited domestic insurrections amongst us, and has endeavoured to bring on the inhabitants of our frontiers, the merciless Indian Savages, whose known rule of warfare, is an undistinguished destruction of all ages, sexes, and conditions.

In every stage of these Oppressions We have Petitioned for Redress in the most humble terms: Our repeated Petitions have been answered only by repeated injury. A Prince, whose character is thus marked by every act which may define a Tyrant, is unfit to be the ruler of a free People.

Nor have We been wanting in attention to our British brethren. We have warned them from time to time of attempts by their legislature to extend an unwarrantable jurisdiction over us. We have reminded them of the circumstances of our emigration and settlement here. We have appealed to their native justice and magnanimity, and we have conjured them by the ties of our common kindred to disavow these usurpations, which would inevitably interrupt our connections and correspondence. They too have been deaf to the voice of justice and of consanguinity. We must, therefore, acquiesce in the necessity, which denounces our Separation, and hold them, as we hold the rest of mankind, Enemies in War, in Peace Friends.

We, THEREFORE the Representatives of the UNITED STATES OF AMERICA, in General Congress, Assembled, appealing to the Supreme Judge of the world for the rectitude of our intentions, do, in the Name, and by Authority of the good People of these Colonies, solemnly publish and declare, That these United Colonies are, and of Right ought to be FREE AND INDEPENDENT STATES; that they are Absolved from all Allegiance to the British Crown, and that all political connection between them and the State of Great Britain, is and ought to be totally dissolved; and that as Free and Independent States, they have full Power to levy War, conclude Peace, contract Alliances, establish Commerce, and to do all other Acts and Things which Independent States may of right do. And for the support of this Declaration, with a firm reliance on the protection of Divine Providence, we mutually pledge to each other our Lives, our Fortunes, and our sacred Honor.

MARTIN LUTHER KING JR.

I Have a Dream

Dr. Martin Luther King Jr. was America's most influential civil rights leader in the mid-twentieth century; he literally laid his life on the line for the beliefs expressed in "I Have a Dream" and "Letter from Birmingham Jail," now contemporary classics. Born in Atlanta (1929) and educated at Morehouse College, King followed his father's calling and was ordained a Baptist clergyman. He quickly gained a reputation for his forceful and charismatic public speaking. At twenty-six King rose to leadership through organizing a successful boycott of the segregated bus system of Montgomery, Alabama. Like Mahatma Gandhi, he was a fervent advocate of nonviolent protests for human rights, particularly of the poor. As the first president of the Southern Christian Leadership Conference, he led numerous sit-ins and demonstrations. Their historic climax was the 1963 march on Washington, D.C. to commemorate Lincoln's Emancipation Proclamation, at which King delivered "I Have a Dream" to 200,000 marchers and one million television viewers. This speech promoted the passage of the 1964 Civil Rights Act and the 1965 Voting Rights Act. King received the Nobel Peace Prize in 1964. Ironically, King's nonviolent practices provoked violence. He was stabbed in New York and stoned in Chicago, and his house in Montgomery was bombed; in 1968 he was assassinated by a sniper. "Free at last," the incantatory phrase that concludes "I Have a Dream," graces his tombstone.

Five score years ago, a great American, in whose symbolic shadow we stand, signed the Emancipation Proclamation. This momentous decree came as a great beacon light of hope to millions of Negro slaves who had been seared in the flames of withering injustice. It came as a joyous daybreak to end the long night of captivity.

But one hundred years later, we must face the tragic fact that the Negro is still not free. One hundred years later, the life of the Negro is still sadly crippled by the manacles of segregation and the chains of discrimination. One hundred years later, the Negro lives on a lonely island of poverty in the midst of a vast ocean of material prosperity. One hundred years later,

---

Martin Luther King Jr., "I Have a Dream" is reprinted by arrangement with The Heirs to the Estate of Martin Luther King Jr., c/o Writers House, Inc. as agent for the proprietor. Copyright 1963 Martin Luther King Jr., renewed 1991 by Coretta Scott King.

the Negro is still languishing in the corners of American society and finds himself an exile in his own land. So we have come here today to dramatize an appalling condition.

In a sense we have come to our nation's capital to cash a check. When the architects of our republic wrote the magnificent words of the Constitution and the Declaration of Independence, they were signing a promissory note to which every American was to fall heir. This note was a promise that all men would be guaranteed the unalienable rights of life, liberty, and the pursuit of happiness.

It is obvious today that America has defaulted on this promissory note insofar as her citizens of color are concerned. Instead of honoring this sacred obligation, America has given the Negro people a bad check; a check which has come back marked "insufficient funds." But we refuse to believe that the bank of justice is bankrupt. We refuse to believe that there are insufficient funds in the great vaults of opportunity of this nation. So we have come to cash this check—a check that will give us upon demand the riches of freedom and the security of justice. We have also come to this hallowed spot to remind America of the fierce urgency of *now*. This is no time to engage in the luxury of cooling off or to take the tranquilizing drugs of gradualism. *Now* is the time to make real the promises of Democracy. *Now* is the time to rise from the dark and desolate valley of segregation to the sunlit path of racial justice. *Now* is the time to open the doors of opportunity to all of God's children. *Now* is the time to lift our nation from the quicksands of racial injustice to the solid rock of brotherhood.

It would be fatal for the nation to overlook the urgency of the moment and to underestimate the determination of the Negro. This sweltering summer of the Negro's legitimate discontent will not pass until there is an invigorating autumn of freedom and equality. 1963 is not an end, but a beginning. Those who hope that the Negro needed to blow off steam and will now be content will have a rude awakening if the nation returns to business as usual. There will be neither rest nor tranquility in America until the Negro is granted his citizenship rights. The whirlwinds of revolt will continue to shake the foundations of our nation until the bright day of justice emerges.

But there is something that I must say to my people who stand on the warm threshold which leads into the palace of justice. In the process of gaining our rightful place we must not be guilty of wrongful deeds. Let us not seek to satisfy our thirst for freedom by drinking from the cup of bitterness and hatred. We must forever conduct our struggle on the high plane of dignity and discipline. We must not allow our creative protest to degenerate into physical violence. Again and again we must rise to the majestic heights of meeting physical force with soul force. The marvelous new militancy which has engulfed the Negro community must not lead us to a distrust of all white people, for many of our white brothers, as evidenced by their presence here today, have come to realize that their destiny is tied up with our destiny and their freedom is inextricably bound to our freedom. We cannot walk alone.

And as we walk, we must make the pledge that we shall march ahead. We cannot turn back. There are those who are asking the devotees of civil rights, "When will you be satisfied?" We can never be satisfied as long as the Negro is the victim of the unspeakable horrors of police brutality. We can never be satisfied as long as our bodies, heavy with the fatigue of travel, cannot gain lodging in the motels of the highways and the hotels of the cities. We cannot be satisfied as long as the Negro's basic mobility is from a smaller ghetto to a larger one. We can never be satisfied as long as a Negro in Mississippi cannot vote and a Negro in New York believes he has nothing for which to vote. No, no, we are not satisfied, and we will not be satisfied until justice rolls down like waters and righteousness like a mighty stream.

I am not unmindful that some of you have come here out of great trials and tribulations. Some of you have come fresh from narrow jail cells. Some of you have come from areas where your quest for freedom left you battered by the storms of persecution and staggered by the winds of police brutality. You have been the veterans of creative suffering. Continue to work with the faith that unearned suffering is redemptive.

Go back to Mississippi, go back to Alabama, go back to South Carolina, go back to Georgia, go back to Louisiana, go back to the slums and ghettos of our northern cities, knowing that somehow this situation can and will be changed. Let us not wallow in the valley of despair.

I say to you today, my friends, that in spite of the difficulties and frustrations of the moment I still have a dream. It is a dream deeply rooted in the American dream.

I have a dream that one day this nation will rise up and live out the true meaning of its creed: "We hold these truths to be self-evident: that all men are created equal."

I have a dream that one day on the red hills of Georgia the sons of former slaves and the sons of former slave owners will be able to sit down together at the table of brotherhood.

I have a dream that one day even the state of Mississippi, a desert state sweltering with the heat of injustice and oppression, will be transformed into an oasis of freedom and justice.

I have a dream that my four little children will one day live in a nation where they will not be judged by the color of their skin but by the content of their character.

I have a dream today.

I have a dream that one day the state of Alabama, whose governor's lips are presently dripping with the words of interposition and nullification, will be transformed into a situation where little black boys and black girls will be able to join hands with little white boys and white girls and walk together as sisters and brothers.

I have a dream today.

I have a dream that one day every valley shall be exalted, every hill and mountain shall be made low, the rough places will be made plain, and the crooked places will be made straight, and the glory of the Lord shall be revealed, and all flesh shall see it together.

This is our hope. This is the faith with which I return to the South. With this faith we will be able to hew out of the mountain of despair a stone of hope. With this faith we will be able to transform the jangling discords of our nation into a beautiful symphony of brotherhood. With this faith we will be able to work together, to pray together, to struggle together, to go to jail together, to stand up for freedom together, knowing that we will be free one day.

This will be the day when all of God's children will be able to sing with new meaning

> My country, 'tis of thee,
> Sweet land of liberty,
>   Of thee I sing:
> Land where my fathers died,
> Land of the pilgrims' pride,
> From every mountainside
>   Let freedom ring.

And if America is to be a great nation this must become true. So let freedom ring from the prodigious hilltops of New Hampshire. Let freedom ring from the mighty mountains of New York. Let freedom ring from the heightening Alleghenies of Pennsylvania!

Let freedom ring from the snowcapped Rockies of Colorado!

Let freedom ring from the curvaceous peaks of California!

But not only that; let freedom ring from Stone Mountain of Georgia!

Let freedom ring from Lookout Mountain of Tennessee!

Let freedom ring from every hill and molehill of Mississippi. From every mountainside, let freedom ring.

When we let freedom ring, when we let it ring from every village and every hamlet, from every state and every city, we will be able to speed up that day when all of God's children, black men and white men, Jews and Gentiles, Protestants and Catholics, will be able to join hands and sing in the words of the old Negro spiritual, "Free at last! free at last! thank God almighty, we are free at last!"

WILLIAM KOWINSKI

Kids in the Mall: Growing Up Controlled

In addition to being the book review and managing arts editor of the *Boston Phoenix*, freelance writer William Kowinski has written for *Esquire*, the *New York Times*, *Smithsonian*, and the *New York Times Magazine*. Kowinski attended Knox College in Illinois and spent one semester at the University of Iowa, where he studied fiction and poetry. He is best known for his 1985 book, *The Malling of America: An Inside Look at the Great Consumer Paradise*, in which "Kids in the Mall" first appeared. In this essay, Kowinski focuses on both the positive and negative aspects of a contemporary phenomenon: the culture of teenagers who spend the majority of their free time in shopping malls, shopping and working while insulating themselves from controlling adults. After exploring whether or not mall life is harmful, Kowinski finally concludes that hanging out in the mall is a learning experience that teaches adolescents "the ways of a large-scale artificial environment: its subtleties and flexibilities" and how to survive in a milieu where "the value system [. . .] is really the dominant one of the whole society."

> Butch heaved himself up and loomed over the group. "Like it was different for me," he piped. "My folks used to drop me off at the shopping mall every morning and leave me all day. It was like a big free baby-sitter, you know? One night they never came back for me. Maybe they moved away. Maybe there's some kind of a Bureau of Missing Parents I could check with."
>
> — RICHARD PECK
> *Secrets of the Shopping Mall*, a
> novel for teenagers

From his sister at Swarthmore, I'd heard about a kid in Florida whose mother picked him up after school every day, drove him straight to the mall, and left him there until it closed—all at his insistence. I'd heard about a boy in Washington who, when his family moved from one suburb

---

William Severini Kowinski, "Kids in the Mall: Growing Up Controlled" from *The Malling of America* by William Severini Kowinski. Copyright © 1985 by William Severini Kowinski. Reprinted by permission of the author.

to another, pedaled his bicycle five miles every day to get back to his old mall, where he once belonged.

These stories aren't unusual. The mall is a common experience for the majority of American youth; they have probably been going there all their lives. Some ran within their first large open space, saw their first fountain, bought their first toy, and read their first book in a mall. They may have smoked their first cigarette or first joint or turned them down, had their first kiss or lost their virginity in the mall parking lot. Teenagers in America now spend more time in the mall than anywhere else but home and school. Mostly it is their choice, but some of that mall time is put in as the result of two-paycheck and single-parent households, and the lack of other viable alternatives. But are these kids being harmed by the mall?

I wondered first of all what difference it makes for adolescents to experience so many important moments in the mall. They are, after all, at play in the fields of its little world and they learn its ways; they adapt to it and make it adapt to them. It's here that these kids get their street sense, only it's mall sense. They are learning the ways of a large-scale artificial environment: its subtleties and flexibilities, its particular pleasures and resonances, and the attitudes it fosters.

The presence of so many teenagers for so much time was not something mall developers planned on. In fact, it came as a big surprise. But kids became a fact of mall life very early, and the International Council of Shopping Centers found it necessary to commission a study, which they published along with a guide to mall managers on how to handle the teenage incursion.

The study found that "teenagers in suburban centers are bored and come to the shopping centers mainly as a place to go. Teenagers in suburban centers spent more time fighting, drinking, littering and walking than did their urban counterparts, but presented fewer overall problems." The report observed that "adolescents congregated in groups of two to four and predominantly at locations selected by them rather than management." This probably had something to do with the decision to install game arcades, which allow management to channel these restless adolescents into naturally contained areas away from major traffic points of adult shoppers.

The guide concluded that mall management should tolerate and even encourage the teenage presence because, in the words of the report, "The vast majority support the same set of values as does shopping center management." *The same set of values* means simply that mall kids are already preprogrammed to be consumers and that the mall can put the finishing touches to them as hard-core, lifelong shoppers just like everybody else. That, after all, is what the mall is about. So it shouldn't be surprising that in spending a lot of time there, adolescents find little that challenges the assumption that the goal of life is to make money and buy products, or that just about everything else in life is to be used to serve those ends.

Growing up in a high-consumption society already adds inestimable pressure to kids' lives. Clothes consciousness has invaded the grade schools, and popularity is linked with having the best, newest clothes in the currently acceptable styles. Even what they read has been affected. "Miss [Nancy] Drew wasn't obsessed with her wardrobe," noted *The Wall Street Journal*. "But today the mystery in teen fiction for girls is what outfit the heroine will wear next." Shopping has become a survival skill and there is certainly no better place to learn it than the mall, where its importance is powerfully reinforced and certainly never questioned.

The mall as a university of suburban materialism, where Valley Girls and Boys from coast to coast are educated in consumption, has its other lessons in this era of change in family life and sexual mores and their economic and social ramifications. The plethora of products in the mall, plus the pressure on teens to buy them, may contribute to the phenomenon that psychologist David Elkin calls "the hurried child": kids who are exposed to too much of the adult world too quickly, and must respond with a sophistication that belies their still-tender emotional development. Certainly the adult products marketed for children—form-fitting designer jeans, sexy tops for preteen girls—add to the social pressure to look like an adult, along with the home-grown need to understand adult finances (why mothers must work) and adult emotions (when parents divorce).

Kids spend so much time at the mall partly because their parents allow it and even encourage it. The mall is safe, it doesn't seem to harbor any unsavory activities, and there is adult supervision; it is, after all, a controlled environment. So the temptation, especially for working parents, is to let the mall be their babysitter. At least the kids aren't watching TV. But the mall's role as a surrogate mother may be more extensive and more profound.

Karen Lansky, a writer living in Los Angeles, has looked into the subject and she told me some of her conclusions about the effects on its teenaged denizens of the mall's controlled and controlling environment. "Structure is the dominant idea, since true 'mall rats' lack just that in their home lives," she said, "and adolescents about to make the big leap into growing up crave more structure than our modern society cares to acknowledge." Karen pointed out some of the elements malls supply that kids used to get from their families, like warmth (Strawberry Shortcake dolls and similar cute and cuddly merchandise), old-fashioned mothering ("We do it all for you," the fast-food slogan), and even home cooking (the "homemade" treats at the food court).

The problem in all this, as Karen Lansky sees it, is that while families nurture children by encouraging growth through the assumption of responsibility and then by letting them rest in the bosom of the family from the rigors of growing up, the mall as a structural mother encourages passivity and consumption, as long as the kid doesn't make trouble. Therefore all they learn about becoming adults is how to act and how to consume.

Kids are in the mall not only in the passive role of shoppers—they also work there, especially as fast-food outlets infiltrate the mall's enclosure. There they learn how to hold a job and take responsibility, but still within the same value context. When *CBS Reports* went to Oak Park Mall in suburban Kansas City, Kansas, to tape part of their hour-long consideration of malls, "After the Dream Comes True," they interviewed a teenaged girl who worked in a fast-food outlet there. In a sequence that didn't make the final program, she described the major goal of her present life, which was to perfect the curl on top of the ice-cream cones that were her store's specialty. If she could do that, she would be moved from the lowly soft-drink dispenser to the more prestigious ice-cream division, the curl on top of the status ladder at her restaurant. These are the achievements that are important at the mall.

Other benefits of such jobs may also be overrated, according to Laurence D. Steinberg of the University of California at Irvine's social ecology department, who did a study on teenage employment. Their jobs, he found, are generally simple, mindlessly repetitive and boring. They don't really learn anything, and the jobs don't lead anywhere. Teenagers also work primarily with other teenagers; even their supervisors are often just a little older than they are. "Kids need to spend time with adults," Steinberg told me. "Although they get benefits from peer relationships, without parents and other adults it's one-sided socialization. They hang out with each other, have age-segregated jobs, and watch TV."

Perhaps much of this is not so terrible or even so terribly different. Now that they have so much more to contend with in their lives, adolescents probably need more time to spend with other adolescents without adult impositions, just to sort things out. Though it is more concentrated in the mall (and therefore perhaps a clearer target), the value system there is really the dominant one of the whole society. Attitudes about curiosity, initiative, self-expression, empathy, and disinterested learning aren't necessarily made in the mall; they are mirrored there, perhaps a bit more intensely—as through a glass brightly.

Besides, the mall is not without its educational opportunities. There are bookstores, where there is at least a short shelf of classics at great prices, and other books from which it is possible to learn more than how to do sit-ups. There are tools, from hammers to VCRs, and products, from clothes to records, that can help the young find and express themselves. There are older people with stories, and places to be alone or to talk one-on-one with a kindred spirit. And there is always the passing show.

The mall itself may very well be an education about the future. I was struck with the realization, as early as my first forays into Greengate, that the mall is only one of a number of enclosed and controlled environments that are part of the lives of today's young. The mall is just an extension, say, of those large suburban schools—only there's Karmelkorn instead of chem lab, the ice rink instead of the gym: It's high school without the impertinence of classes.

Growing up, moving from home to school to the mall—from enclosure to enclosure, transported in cars—is a curiously continuous process, without much in the way of contrast or contact with unenclosed reality. Places must tend to blur into one another. But whatever differences and dangers there are in this, the skills these adolescents are learning may turn out to be useful in their later lives. For we seem to be moving inexorably into an age of preplanned and regulated environments, and this is the world they will inherit.

Still, it might be better if they had more of a choice. One teenaged girl confessed to *CBS Reports* that she sometimes felt she was missing something by hanging out at the mall so much. "But I'm here," she said, "and this is what I have."

BRENT STAPLES

Black Men and Public Space

Brent Staples was born in a "small, angry industrial town" in Pennsylvania in 1951. When the town's prosperity declined and family problems developed, his family (which included eight siblings) moved, and kept moving to avoid creditors. Despite this chaotic childhood, Staples finished high school and was admitted to Widener University with several other black students as part of a special program. He earned a B.A. in behavioral science (1973), which was followed by a Ph.D. in psychology at the University of Chicago (1977). He has worked as a lecturer at several colleges, and since 1983, as an editorial writer for the *New York Times*. To Staples, the term "the black experience" oversimplifies the variety of experiences among African Americans. His autobiography, *Parallel Time: Growing Up in Black and White* (1994), invokes the kind of complex events that, he insists, people of all races share: family life, leaving home, and developing an individual identity. "Black Men and Public Space" (*Harper's*, 1986), however, focuses on his experiences of racism. Speaking as if he were a racist, Staples ironically explains that strangers anticipate "nastiness" and even criminal behavior when passing a lone black man on a dark street. To counter his ability to "alter public space in ugly ways," he writes with dry humor, noting that he has learned to whistle Vivaldi melodies while walking at night, his "equivalent of the cowbell that hikers wear when they know they are in bear country."

My first victim was a woman—white, well dressed, probably in her early twenties. I came upon her late one evening on a deserted street in Hyde Park, a relatively affluent neighborhood in an otherwise mean, impoverished section of Chicago. As I swung onto the avenue behind her, there seemed to be a discreet, uninflammatory distance between us. Not so. She cast back a worried glance. To her, the youngish black man—a broad six feet two inches with a beard and billowing hair, both hands shoved into the pockets of a bulky military jacket—seemed menacingly close. After a few more quick glimpses, she picked up her pace and was soon running in earnest. Within seconds she disappeared into a cross street.

Brent Staples, "Black Men and Public Space" from *Harper's* magazine, December 1986. Reprinted by permission of the author.

That was more than a decade ago. I was twenty-two years old, a graduate student newly arrived at the University of Chicago. It was in the echo of that terrified woman's footfalls that I first began to know the unwieldy inheritance I'd come into — the ability to alter public space in ugly ways. It was clear that she thought herself the quarry of a mugger, a rapist, or worse. Suffering a bout of insomnia, however, I was stalking sleep, not defenseless wayfarers. As a softy who is scarcely able to take a knife to a raw chicken — let alone hold one to a person's throat — I was surprised, embarrassed, and dismayed all at once. Her flight made me feel like an accomplice in tyranny. It also made it clear that I was indistinguishable from the muggers who occasionally seeped into the area from the surrounding ghetto. That first encounter, and those that followed, signified that a vast, unnerving gulf lay between nighttime pedestrians — particularly women — and me. And I soon gathered that being perceived as dangerous is a hazard in itself. I only needed to turn a corner into a dicey situation, or crowd some frightened, armed person in a foyer somewhere, or make an errant move after being pulled over by a policeman. Where fear and weapons meet — and they often do in urban America — there is always the possibility of death.

In that first year, my first away from my hometown, I was to become thoroughly familiar with the language of fear. At dark, shadowy intersections, I could cross in front of a car stopped at a traffic light and elicit the *thunk, thunk, thunk, thunk* of the driver — black, white, male, or female — hammering down the door locks. On less traveled streets after dark, I grew accustomed to but never comfortable with people crossing to the other side of the street rather than pass me. Then there were the standard unpleasantries with policemen, doormen, bouncers, cabdrivers, and others whose business it is to screen out troublesome individuals *before* there is any nastiness.

I moved to New York nearly two years ago and I have remained an avid night walker. In central Manhattan, the near-constant crowd cover minimizes tense one-on-one street encounters. Elsewhere — in SoHo, for example, where sidewalks are narrow and tightly spaced buildings shut out the sky — things can get very taut indeed.

After dark, on the warrenlike streets of Brooklyn where I live, I often see women who fear the worst from me. They seem to have set their faces on neutral, and with their purse straps strung across their chests bandolier-style, they forge ahead as though bracing themselves against being tackled. I understand, of course, that the danger they perceive is not a hallucination. Women are particularly vulnerable to street violence, and young black males are drastically overrepresented among the perpetrators of that violence. Yet these truths are no solace against the kind of alienation that comes of being ever the suspect, a fearsome entity with whom pedestrians avoid making eye contact.

It is not altogether clear to me how I reached the ripe old age of twenty-two without being conscious of the lethality nighttime pedestrians attributed to me. Perhaps it was because in Chester, Pennsylvania, the small, angry industrial town where I came of age in the 1960s, I was scarcely noticeable against a backdrop of gang warfare, street knifings, and murders. I grew up one of the good boys, had perhaps a half-dozen fistfights. In retrospect, my shyness of combat has clear sources.

As a boy, I saw countless tough guys locked away; I have since buried several, too. They were babies, really—a teenage cousin, a brother of twenty-two, a childhood friend in his mid-twenties—all gone down in episodes of bravado played out in the streets. I came to doubt the virtues of intimidation early on. I chose, perhaps unconsciously, to remain a shadow—timid, but a survivor.

The fearsomeness mistakenly attributed to me in public places often has a perilous flavor. The most frightening of these confusions occurred in the late 1970s and early 1980s, when I worked as a journalist in Chicago. One day, rushing into the office of a magazine I was writing for with a deadline story in hand, I was mistaken for a burglar. The office manager called security and, with an ad hoc posse, pursued me through the labyrinthine halls, nearly to my editor's door. I had no way of proving who I was. I could only move briskly toward the company of someone who knew me.

Another time I was on assignment for a local paper and killing time before an interview. I entered a jewelry store on the city's affluent Near North Side. The proprietor excused herself and returned with an enormous red Doberman pinscher straining at the end of a leash. She stood, the dog extended toward me, silent to my questions, her eyes bulging nearly out of her head. I took a cursory look around, nodded, and bade her good night.

Relatively speaking, however, I never fared as badly as another black male journalist. He went to nearby Waukegan, Illinois, a couple of summers ago to work on a story about a murderer who was born there. Mistaking the reporter for the killer, police officers hauled him from his car at gunpoint and but for his press credentials would probably have tried to book him. Such episodes are not uncommon. Black men trade tales like this all the time.

Over the years, I learned to smother the rage I felt at so often being taken for a criminal. Not to do so would surely have led to madness. I now take precautions to make myself less threatening. I move about with care, particularly late in the evening. I give a wide berth to nervous people on subway platforms during the wee hours, particularly when I have exchanged business clothes for jeans. If I happen to be entering a building behind some people who appear skittish, I may walk by, letting them clear the lobby before I return, so as not to seem to be following them. I have been calm and extremely congenial on those rare occasions when I've been pulled over by the police.

And on late-evening constitutionals I employ what has proved to be an excellent tension-reducing measure: I whistle melodies from Beethoven and Vivaldi and the more popular classical composers. Even steely New Yorkers hunching toward nighttime destinations seem to relax, and occasionally they even join in the tune. Virtually everybody seems to sense that a mugger wouldn't be warbling bright, sunny selections from Vivaldi's *Four Seasons*. It is my equivalent of the cowbell that hikers wear when they know they are in bear country.

DEBORAH TANNEN

Sex, Lies, and Conversation

>   Deborah Tannen was born in Brooklyn in 1945. Her interest in the "language of everyday conversation" led her to study linguistics at the University of California–Berkeley (Ph.D., 1979) and to her professorship at Georgetown University. A contributor to many linguistics journals, popular magazines, and newspapers, Tannen has also won prizes for poetry and short stories (*Greek Icons*, 1978). An expert on communication in the workplace, Tannen explores the ways in which gender and cultural differences influence linguistic styles. She attributes her cross-cultural approach in part to years spent teaching English in Greece. In her best-sellers, *That's Not What I Meant! How Conversational Styles Make or Break Your Relations with Others* (1986), and *Talking from 9 to 5* (1994), she explains how misunderstandings can lead to communication breakdown. Her most recent book is *The Argument Culture* (1998). In "Sex, Lies, and Conversation," from *You Just Don't Understand: Women and Men in Conversation* (1990), Tannen compares and contrasts conversational differences between men and women, differences that arise in childhood through socialization. Through interviews with married couples and analyses of videotaped conversations between same-sex friends, Tannen finds that communication problems between the sexes require a "cross-cultural understanding" as a path to harmony.

   I was addressing a small gathering in a suburban Virginia living room — a women's group that had invited men to join them. Throughout the evening, one man had been particularly talkative, frequently offering ideas and anecdotes, while his wife sat silently beside him on the couch. Toward the end of the evening, I commented that women frequently complain that their husbands don't talk to them. This man quickly concurred. He gestured toward his wife and said, "She's the talker in our family." The room burst into laughter; the man looked puzzled and hurt. "It's true," he explained. "When I come home from work I have nothing to say. If she didn't keep the conversation going, we'd spend the whole evening in silence."

Deborah Tannen, "Sex, Lies, and Conversation" from *You Just Don't Understand* by Deborah Tannen. Copyright © 1990 by Deborah Tannen. Reprinted by permission of HarperCollins Publishers, Inc. Originally published in *The Washington Post*, June 24, 1990. Copyright Deborah Tannen. Reprinted by permission of the author.

This episode crystallizes the irony that although American men tend to talk more than women in public situations, they often talk less at home. And this pattern is wreaking havoc with marriage.

The pattern was observed by political scientist Andrew Hacker in the late seventies. Sociologist Catherine Kohler Riessman reports in her new book *Divorce Talk* that most of the women she interviewed—but only a few of the men—gave lack of communication as the reason for their divorces. Given the current divorce rate of nearly 50 percent, that amounts to millions of cases in the United States every year—a virtual epidemic of failed conversation.

In my own research, complaints from women about their husbands most often focused not on tangible inequities such as having given up the chance for a career to accompany a husband to his, or doing far more than their share of daily life-support work like cleaning, cooking, social arrangements and errands. Instead, they focused on communication: "He doesn't listen to me," "He doesn't talk to me." I found, as Hacker observed years before, that most wives want their husbands to be, first and foremost, conversational partners, but few husbands share this expectation of their wives.

In short, the image that best represents the current crisis is the stereotypical cartoon scene of a man sitting at the breakfast table with a newspaper held up in front of his face, while a woman glares at the back of it, wanting to talk.

Linguistic Battle of the Sexes

How can women and men have such different impressions of communication in marriage? Why the widespread imbalance in their interests and expectations?

In the April issue of *American Psychologist,* Stanford University's Eleanor Maccoby reports the results of her own and others' research showing that children's development is most influenced by the social structure of peer interactions. Boys and girls tend to play with children of their own gender, and their sex-separate groups have different organizational structures and interactive norms.

I believe these systematic differences in childhood socialization make talk between women and men like cross-cultural communication, heir to all the attraction and pitfalls of that enticing but difficult enterprise. My research on men's and women's conversations uncovered patterns similar to those described for children's groups.

For women, as for girls, intimacy is the fabric of relationships, and talk is the thread from which it is woven. Little girls create and maintain friendships by exchanging secrets; similarly, women regard conversation as the cornerstone of friendship. So a woman expects her husband to be a new and improved version of a best friend. What is important is not the individual subjects that are discussed but the sense of closeness, of a life shared, that emerges when people tell their thoughts, feelings, and impressions.

Bonds between boys can be as intense as girls', but they are based less on talking, more on doing things together. Since they don't assume talk is the cement that binds a relationship, men don't know what kind of talk women want, and they don't miss it when it isn't there.

Boys' groups are larger, more inclusive, and more hierarchical, so boys must struggle to avoid the subordinate position in the group. This may play a role in women's complaints that men don't listen to them. Some men really don't like to listen, because being the listener makes them feel one-down, like a child listening to adults or an employee to a boss.

But often when women tell men, "You aren't listening," and the men protest, "I am," the men are right. The impression of not listening results from misalignments in the mechanics of conversation. The misalignment begins as soon as a man and a woman take physical positions. This became clear when I studied videotapes made by psychologist Bruce Dorval of children and adults talking to their same-sex best friends. I found that at every age, the girls and women faced each other directly, their eyes anchored on each other's faces. At every age, the boys and men sat at angles to each other and looked elsewhere in the room, periodically glancing at each other. They were obviously attuned to each other, often mirroring each other's movements. But the tendency of men to face away can give women the impression they aren't listening even when they are. A young woman in college was frustrated: Whenever she told her boyfriend she wanted to talk to him, he would lie down on the floor, close his eyes, and put his arm over his face. This signaled to her, "He's taking a nap." But he insisted he was listening extra hard. Normally, he looks around the room, so he is easily distracted. Lying down and covering his eyes helped him concentrate on what she was saying.

Analogous to the physical alignment that women and men take in conversation is their topical alignment. The girls in my study tended to talk at length about one topic, but the boys tended to jump from topic to topic. The second-grade girls exchanged stories about people they knew. The second-grade boys teased, told jokes, noticed things in the room, and talked about finding games to play. The sixth-grade girls talked about problems with a mutual friend. The sixth-grade boys talked about fifty-five different topics, none of which extended over more than a few turns.

Listening to Body Language

Switching topics is another habit that gives women the impression men aren't listening, especially if they switch to a topic about themselves. But the evidence of the tenth-grade boys in my study indicates otherwise. The tenth-grade boys sprawled across their chairs with bodies parallel and eyes straight ahead, rarely looking at each other. They looked as if they were riding in a car, staring out the windshield. But they were talking about their feelings. One boy was upset because a girl had told him he had a drinking problem, and the other was feeling alienated from all his friends.

Now, when a girl told a friend about a problem, the friend responded by asking probing questions and expressing agreement and understanding. But the boys dismissed each other's problems. Todd assured Richard that his drinking was "no big problem" because "sometimes you're funny when you're off your butt." And when Todd said he felt left out, Richard responded, "Why should you? You know more people than me."

Women perceive such responses as belittling and unsupportive. But the boys seemed satisfied with them. Whereas women reassure each other by implying, "You shouldn't feel bad because I've had similar experiences," men do so by implying, "You shouldn't feel bad because your problems aren't so bad."

There are even simpler reasons for women's impression that men don't listen. Linguist Lynette Hirschman found that women make more listener-noise, such as "mhm," "uhuh," and "yeah," to show "I'm with you." Men, she found, more often give silent attention. Women who expect a stream of listener-noise interpret silent attention as no attention at all.

Women's conversational habits are as frustrating to men as men's are to women. Men who expect silent attention interpret a stream of listener-noise as overreaction or impatience. Also, when women talk to each other in a close, comfortable setting, they often overlap, finish each other's sentences, and anticipate what the other is about to say. This practice, which I call "participatory listenership," is often perceived by men as interruption, intrusion, and lack of attention.

A parallel difference caused a man to complain about his wife, "She just wants to talk about her own point of view. If I show her another view, she gets mad at me." When most women talk to each other, they assume a conversationalist's job is to express agreement and support. But many men see their conversational duty as pointing out the other side of an argument. This is heard as disloyalty by women, and refusal to offer the requisite support. It is not that women don't want to see other points of view, but that they prefer them phrased as suggestions and inquiries rather than as direct challenges.

In his book *Fighting for Life*, Walter Ong points out that men use "agonistic" or warlike, oppositional formats to do almost anything; thus discussion becomes debate, and conversation a competitive sport. In contrast, women see conversation as a ritual means of establishing rapport. If Jane tells a problem and June says she has a similar one, they walk away feeling closer to each other. But this attempt at establishing rapport can backfire when used with men. Men take too literally women's ritual "troubles talk," just as women mistake men's ritual challenges for real attack.

The Sounds of Silence

These differences begin to clarify why women and men have such different expectations about communication in marriage. For women, talk creates intimacy. Marriage is an orgy of closeness: you can tell your feelings and thoughts, and still be loved. Their greatest fear is being pushed away. But men live in a hierarchical world, where talk maintains independence and status. They are on guard to protect themselves from being put down and pushed around.

This explains the paradox of the talkative man who said of his silent wife, "She's the talker." In the public setting of a guest lecture, he felt challenged to show his intelligence and display his understanding of the lecture. But at home, where he has nothing to prove and no one to defend against, he is free to remain silent. For his wife, being home means she is free from the worry that something she says might offend someone, or spark disagreement, or appear to be showing off; at home she is free to talk.

The communication problems that endanger marriage can't be fixed by mechanical engineering. They require a new conceptual framework about the role of talk in human relationships. Many of the psychological explanations that have become second nature may not be helpful, because they tend to blame either women (for not being assertive enough) or men (for not being in touch with their feelings). A sociolinguistic approach by which male-female conversation is seen as cross-cultural communication allows us to understand the problem and forge solutions without blaming either party.

Once the problem is understood, improvement comes naturally, as it did to the young woman and her boyfriend who seemed to go to sleep when she wanted to talk. Previously, she had accused him of not listening, and he had refused to change his behavior, since that would be admitting fault. But then she learned about and explained to him the differences in women's and men's habitual ways of aligning themselves in conversation. The next time she told him she wanted to talk, he began, as usual, by lying down and covering his eyes. When the familiar negative reaction bubbled up, she reassured herself that he really was listening. But then he sat up and looked at her. Thrilled, she asked why. He said, "You like me to look at you when we talk, so I'll try to do it." Once he saw their differences as cross-cultural rather than right and wrong, he independently altered his behavior.

Women who feel abandoned and deprived when their husbands won't listen to or report daily news may be happy to discover their husbands trying to adapt once they understand the place of small talk in women's relationships. But if their husbands don't adapt, the women may still be comforted that for men, this is not a failure of intimacy. Accepting the difference, the wives may look to their friends or family for that kind of talk. And husbands who can't provide it shouldn't feel their wives have made unreasonable demands. Some couples will still decide to divorce, but at least their decisions will be based on realistic expectations.

In these times of resurgent ethnic conflicts, the world desperately needs cross-cultural understanding. Like charity, successful cross-cultural communication should begin at home.